**Genre** Realistic Fi

MW00570691

 Essential Question
How do people figure things out?

Two Up, One Down

by Frederica Brown
illustrated by Mark Weber

Chapter 1 Trouble at Practice

May wheeled herself to the other side of the court as fast as she could, but she missed the ball. It bounced outside the line.

"Oh no!" she cried in frustration. "That's the sixth ball I've missed today! I just can't reach the ball by the second bounce!"

"Calm down," said her coach, Paul. "It's important not to let your temper get the better of you, especially in a sport like tennis. You just need to get more practice in between your lessons with me. Is there someone you can play with?"

"No," said May gloomily. "I can't think of anyone."

As they drove home after the lesson, May told her mother about needing someone to practice with. "I can't imagine how I'm ever going to get better if I can't practice," she said. "I want to be a really good tennis player."

Mom was a careful observer of May's tennis lessons. "I could practice with you," she said.

"That would be great, Mom," said May. But May was doubtful. Her mother was not very athletic, and she didn't play tennis very often.

The next day, May and her mother went to the tennis courts after school to practice.

"Don't forget, Mom, the ball is allowed to bounce twice in wheelchair tennis," May said as she took her position on the other side of the net. "Give me some easy hits to start with. I'll work on my style."

May's mother hit the ball, and May returned it on the second bounce. Mom swung her racket wildly and missed it.

"Sorry!" she called as she went running after the ball.

May sighed as she waited for her mother to get the ball. Her mom hit the ball to her again. May returned it on the second bounce, and this time her mother managed to hit the ball back over the net. May returned the ball with a strong backhand stroke that her mother couldn't reach. As her mom went to pick up the ball, May called, "Just leave it, Mom! We can pick up the balls later. Use another one. There's a can of balls in my sports bag!"

"Oh, I didn't think of that," said her mother. "What a good idea." She opened the can of tennis balls.

May met her mother at the net. "Could you give me a few balls as well, please?" she asked. "I'll put them into the spokes of my wheels. That will speed things up a bit. Paul says that when I'm on the court, I should never stop moving. But I'm finding it hard to do that today."

"I'm doing my best," said her mother, looking flustered. "Are you ready? Let's try again."

The practice went a little better after that. May kept her temper, and her mother managed to return three shots in a row. But then she missed a few, and May felt her temper rise again. Then her mother hit the ball so wildly that it landed in the next court, where another girl was training with her coach.

May threw her tennis racket to the ground in anger as her mother went off to get the ball.

When she came back, May's mother looked at her daughter. May's face was as red as a hot coal. Her mother decided it was time for a breather.

"Let's take a break," she said. "I'll get some water from the car."

May waited glumly for the water. For something to do, she watched the pair that her mother had interrupted on the next court.

The girl looked about her own age, which was thirteen. Her coach was sending her balls that looked easy enough to return, except that they were all over the court. The girl was fierce in chasing down every ball. She never stopped moving, and she managed to return a few balls that May thought looked impossible.

"But she misses some, too," thought May, as the girl didn't quite reach one. Then May had an idea for a new way to practice.

When May's mother came back with water bottles, May apologized for getting mad.

Then she added, "But I think I might have a solution to our problem.

"I was watching that girl over there while you were at the car," said May. "Her coach has a pile of balls and just hits them to her one after the other, first to the left, then to the right. Can we try it like that?"

Mom hit the first ball to the back right of the court, then to the back left, then to the back right again. May struggled to change direction quickly enough to reach the ball by the second bounce. She missed more than she hit at first. But she was determined to keep going. Gradually, she was able to return almost every ball. She never stopped moving, just as Paul had instructed. It felt great.

May had just returned her third ball in a row when she realized she had an observer. The girl on the next court was watching her and smiling.

"Hi, I'm Jenna," she said, coming over. "I was watching you practice. I really like the way you use the momentum of your wheelchair to give power to your shots. You can make the ball spin like a top! Do you want to have a few hits?"

May was about to say yes when her mother said, "We need to head home soon. Why don't you two cool down now?"

"Okay, Mom," said May. "Next time, I'd love to," she said to Jenna.

As the girls did their stretches, they talked.

"My favorite player is Roger Federer," said Jenna. "He's incredible! I hope I can play like him one day."

"Esther Vergeer is my hero," said May.

"I've never heard of her," said Jenna. "What tournaments has she won?"

"Esther Vergeer has been the number one wheelchair tennis player for more than ten years," said May. "She's a fantastic player. Watching her inspired me to take up tennis in the first place."

"Wow," said Jenna. "I'd like to watch her play."

"I've got a DVD of some of her matches," said May. "Maybe you'd like to come and watch it with me some time?"

"Sure, that would be great," said Jenna. "How about tomorrow?"

Jenna came over after school, and May put the DVD on. They watched Esther Vergeer playing in a U.S. Open Wheelchair final. Jenna was impressed by Vergeer's skill. "Are there any other players you like?" she asked May.

"A few," said May. "But check out this game of doubles."

She played a video clip on the computer. "It's called 'One Up, One Down,'" she said. "The team is made up of one able-bodied player and one wheelchair player."

"That looks like fun!" said Jenna. "We should practice together."

"That would be great," said May, smiling.

On the weekend, May's mother took the girls to the tennis courts. "I'm glad you two are going to practice together," she said. "Tennis is not really my sport."

May giggled. "You can say that again, Mom."

Jenna took one side of the net and May the other. Things started off well as the girls hit to one another. But as they warmed up, Jenna started to hit the ball harder and faster. May was having a hard time returning all of them. She felt frustrated as she missed one, then two balls.

"Hey, Jenna," she called. "Time out, please!"

May wheeled herself up to the net.

"I don't want you to go easy on me," she said
to Jenna. "But sometimes I need you to give me
a slow ball so I can get into the right position.
It's hard to hold my racket and move my wheels
at the same time."

"Sorry," said Jenna. "I'll try to make some slow
and some fast."

May's mother came over to them with water bottles. "How is it going?" she asked.

Suddenly May had a good idea.

"Mom, remember how every ball you hit seems to come at me in slow motion?" May asked. "Why don't you and Jenna take turns hitting balls to me?"

"That's a great idea!" said Jenna.

May's mom ran to get a tennis racket and took her place at Jenna's end of the court. She hit a slow ball. Then Jenna hit a fast one to the same side of the court, where May was ready. Then they both hit to the other side.

It worked well. May got much better at returning Jenna's powerful shots, and Jenna's accuracy improved. They all had a lot of fun.

"You're the inventor of a new game, May," said Jenna when they had finished. "'Two Up, One Down!'"

Summarize

Use details from the story to summarize *Two Up, One Down*. Your Point of View chart may help you.

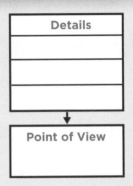

Details

Point of View

Text Evidence

1. What kind of fiction is *Two Up, One Down*? Which details tell you this? GENRE

2. What happens to change May's point of view in *Two Up, One Down*? What clues can you find in the text to support your answer? POINT OF VIEW

3. What simile does the author use on page 9? Which words helped you find it? SIMILES

4. Write about how May in *Two Up, One Down* changes from the beginning to the end of the story. WRITE ABOUT READING

Compare Texts
Read how people and animals find what they need.

I Listen

If I need to talk
I listen to the wind
The wind whispers
and we share secrets together

If I want to dance
I listen to the sea
The sea beats out a rhythm
and we dance together

If I can't sleep
I listen to the rain
The rain sings me to sleep
and we dream together

The Nesting Box

Grandpa made the nesting box
For the bluebirds, he said.
A small front door
A round front door.

From my bed, I spy a bluebird
Sky blue and rusty red
At his small front door
At his round front door.

He holds a long piece of straw
He tries the straw this way
He tries the straw that way
Too long for his small front door.

I wonder if he'll fly away?
To find another piece of straw
A piece that fits his front door

But no, the bluebird turns around
He slides the straw sideways
Into his small front door
Into his round front door

He puffs up his feathers
Sky blue and rusty red
And I think,
I must phone Grandpa.

Make Connections

What problems is the speaker of the poem "I Listen"
solving by listening to the wind, the ocean, and the
rain? ESSENTIAL QUESTION

What comparison can you make between the bird
in "The Nesting Box" and May in *Two Up, One Down*?
TEXT TO TEXT

Focus on
Literary Elements

Rhyme Poems often use literary elements such as *rhyme* and *alliteration*. Rhyme is the repetition of a similar sound at the end of two or more words. An example of rhyme is, *We'll meet you, At the zoo.* Alliteration is the repetition of the consonant at the beginning of two or more words that are next to one another. An example is, *a wet, windy, and wild day.*

Read and Find The poem *I Listen* is written in free verse. It uses repetition to create rhythm. Read the poem aloud to hear the rhythm clearly. The poem *The Nesting Box* creates rhythm with the repetition of words such as *straw* and *door.*

Your Turn

Write your own poem. You can make it rhyme or use free verse. Try to add some alliteration, too.